Coloring Book for Adults

15 ANTI-STRESS COLORING PATTERNS

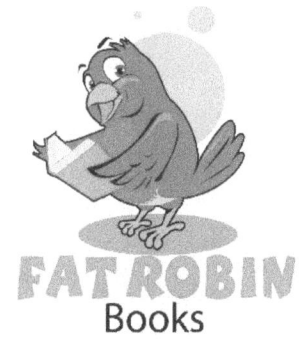

FAT ROBIN
Books

We encourage the purchaser of this book to make photocopies of these patterns, for their own personal (family!) use, but for anything else, please obtain the express written permission of the publisher prior to reproducing the contents of this book for any other means.

Introduction

Thank-you for downloading this book which contains 15 Unique Adult Coloring Patterns.

You can also get a PDF version of these patterns so you can print them out again (and again?) if someone in the family gets to them first!

Just Checkout the Link at the back of this book!

How to use this book?

That's really up to you but we think you have 2 options!

Option 1: Flick through the book, find a pattern you like, print it out and get coloring!

Option 2: Like with any fun activity, it's worth taking precautions and a picture does paint a thousand words, so…

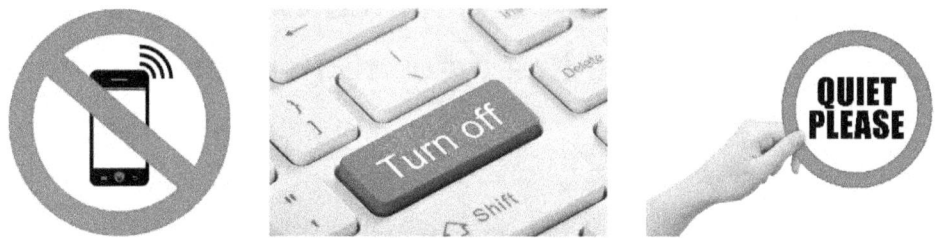

Then add some or all of these:

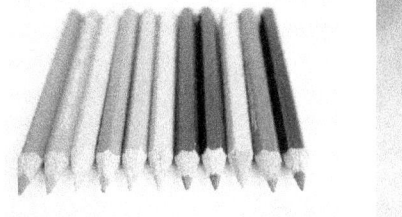 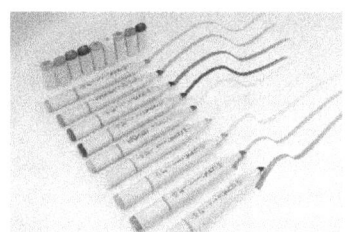 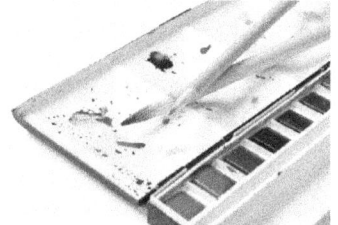

And finally…flick through the book, find a pattern you like, print it out and get coloring!

Top Tips:

- Placing a piece of paper (or card) under the pattern you're coloring in will stop any 'ink' bleeding through between pages.

- Each pattern is printed on one side of paper only making these ideal to remove from the book, keep for yourself or give as a gift (they'd look lovely in a frame!).

- Enjoy yourself and leave any stress behind.

Looking for more Adult Coloring Books?

Also available from Fat Robin Books:

Coloring Book for Adults: Volume 1 - Tranquility

Coloring Book for Adults: Volume 2 – Serenity

Coloring Book for Adults: Volume 3 – Harmony

Coloring Book for Adults: Volume 4 – Symmetry

Coloring Book for Adults: Volume 5 - Simplicity

Each Volume contains 50 Superbly detailed Coloring Patterns for Adults, and each Volume has its own distinctive theme

How about also showing off your great work?

Checkout:

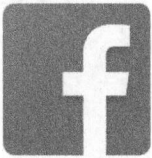

Facebook:

www.FatRobinBooks.com/Facebook-Page

www.FatRobinBooks.com/Pinterest

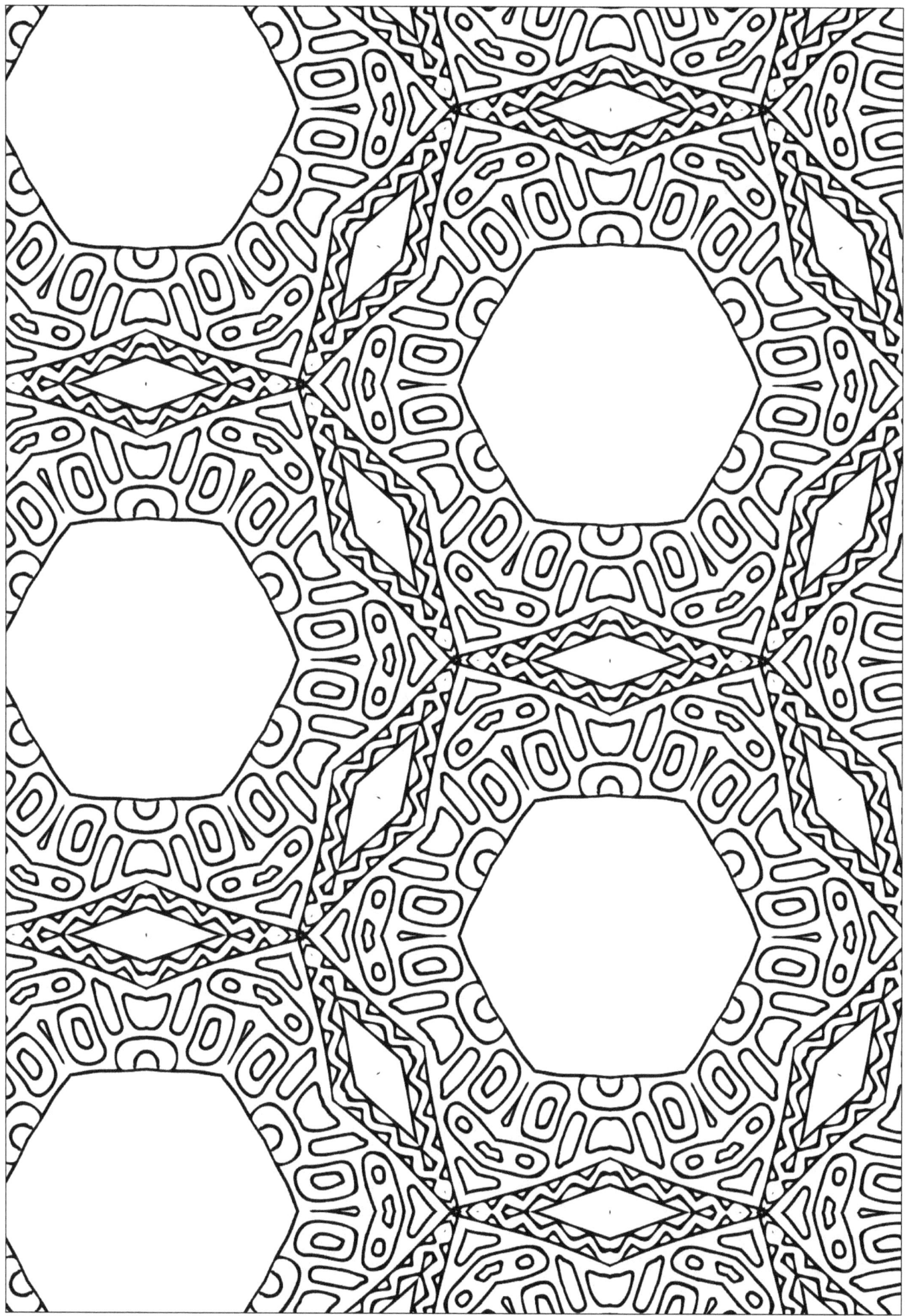

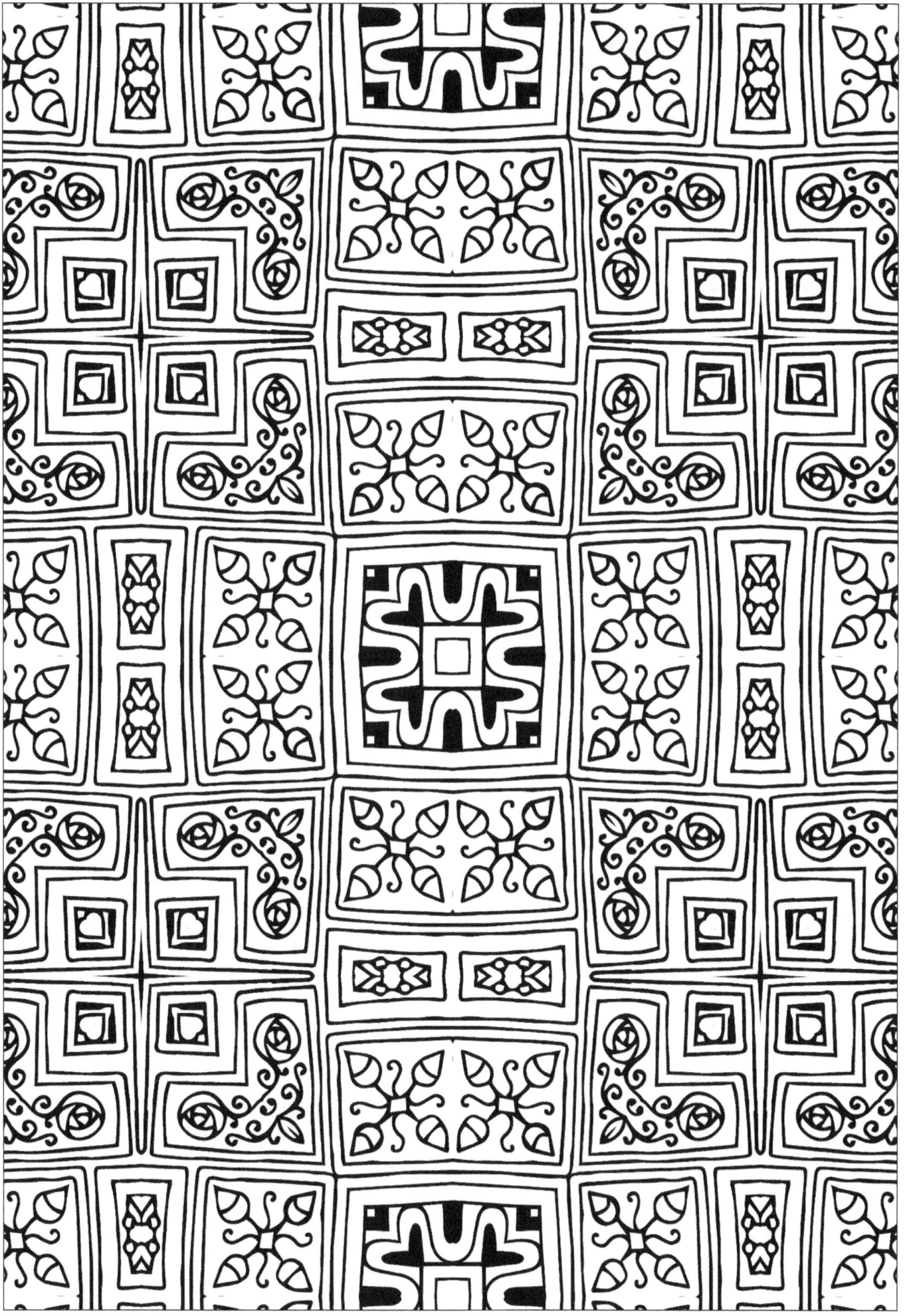

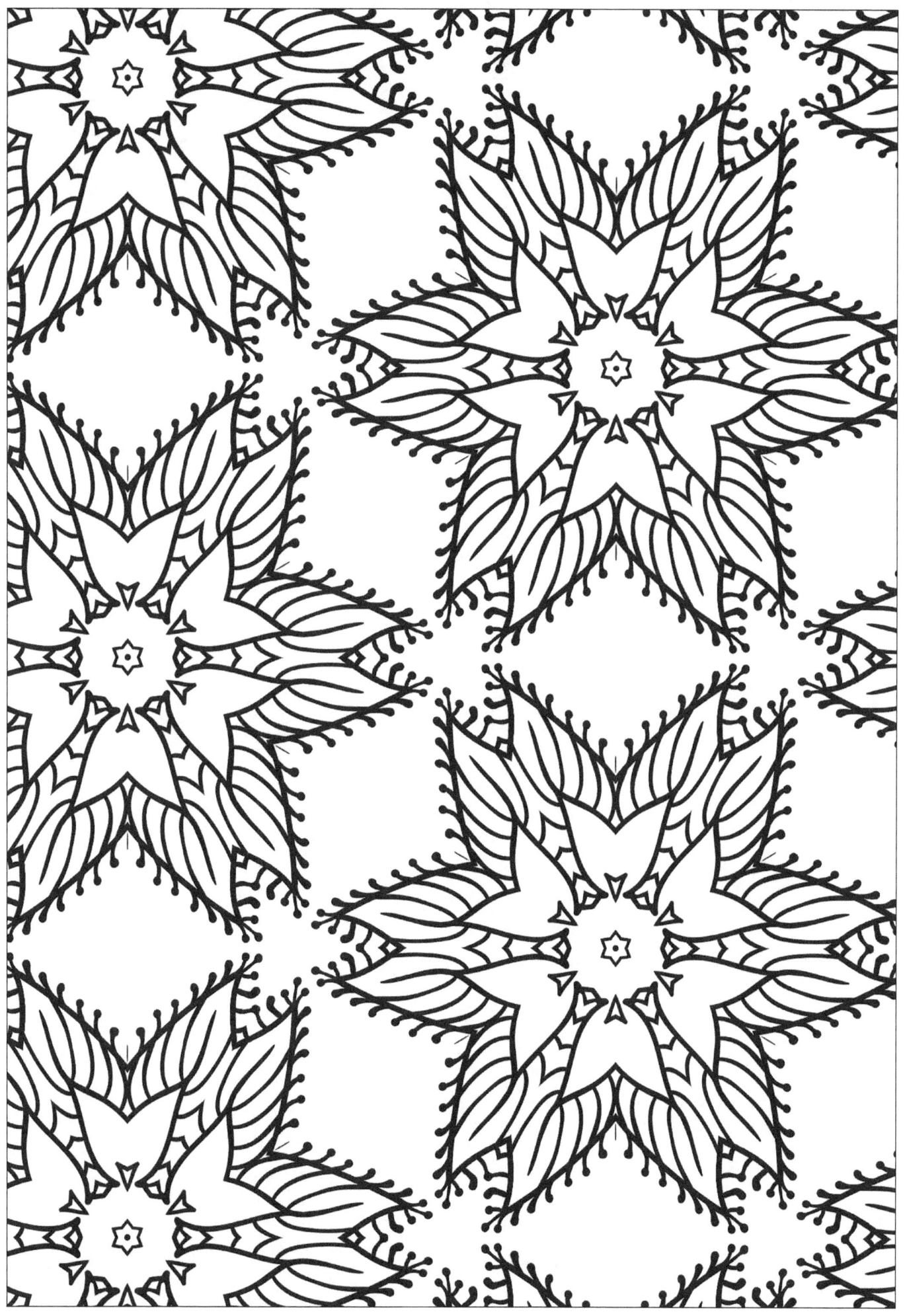

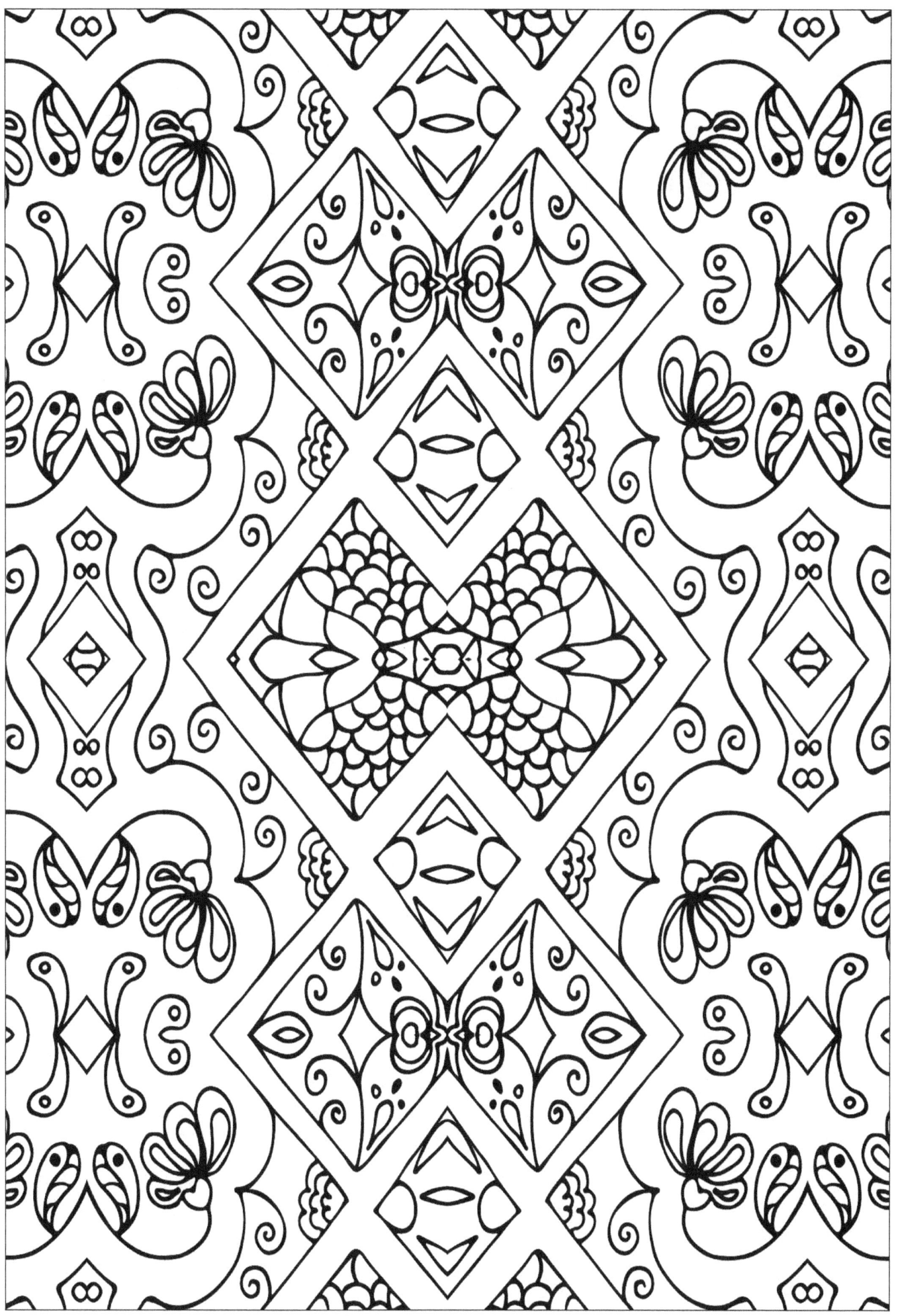

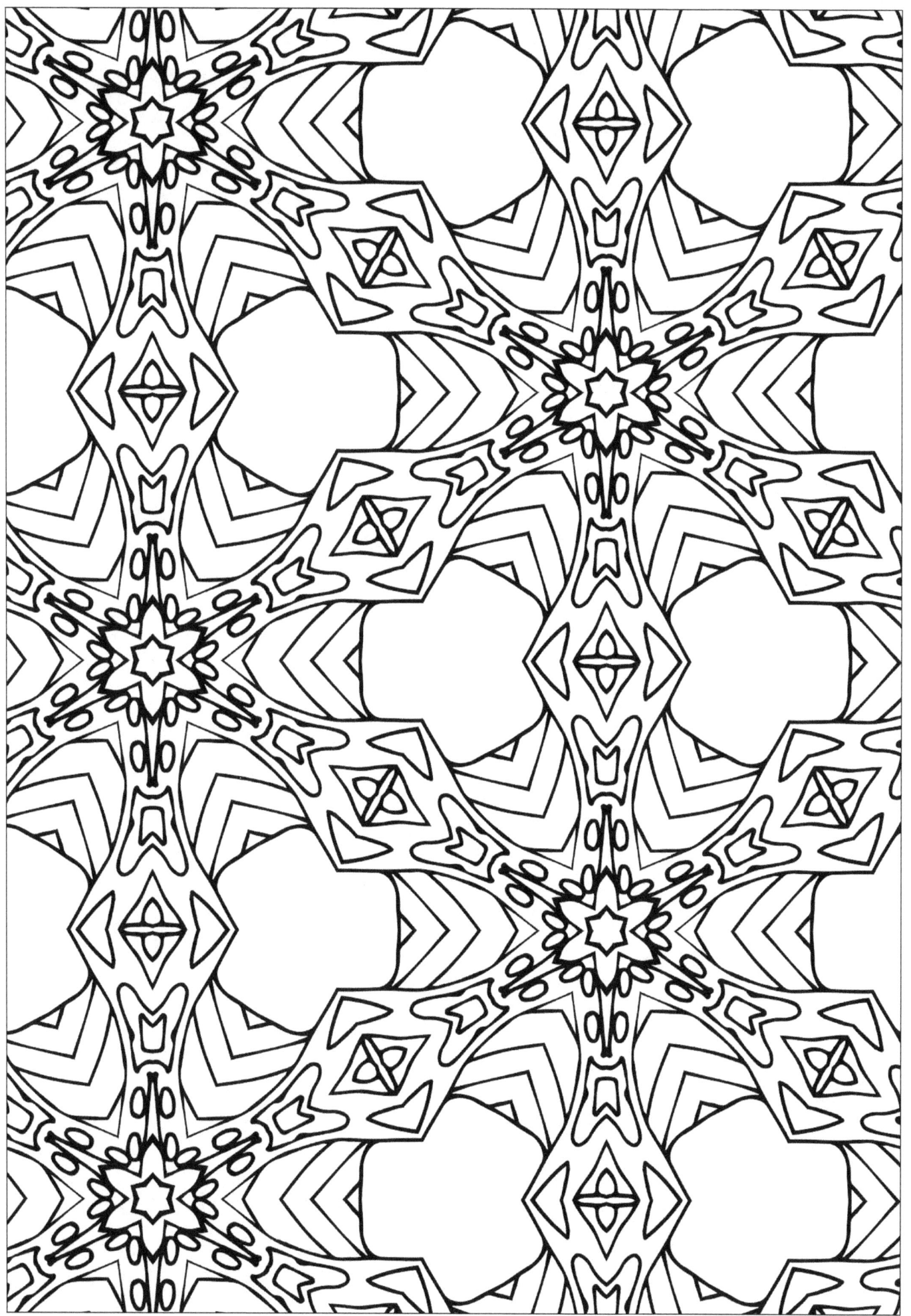

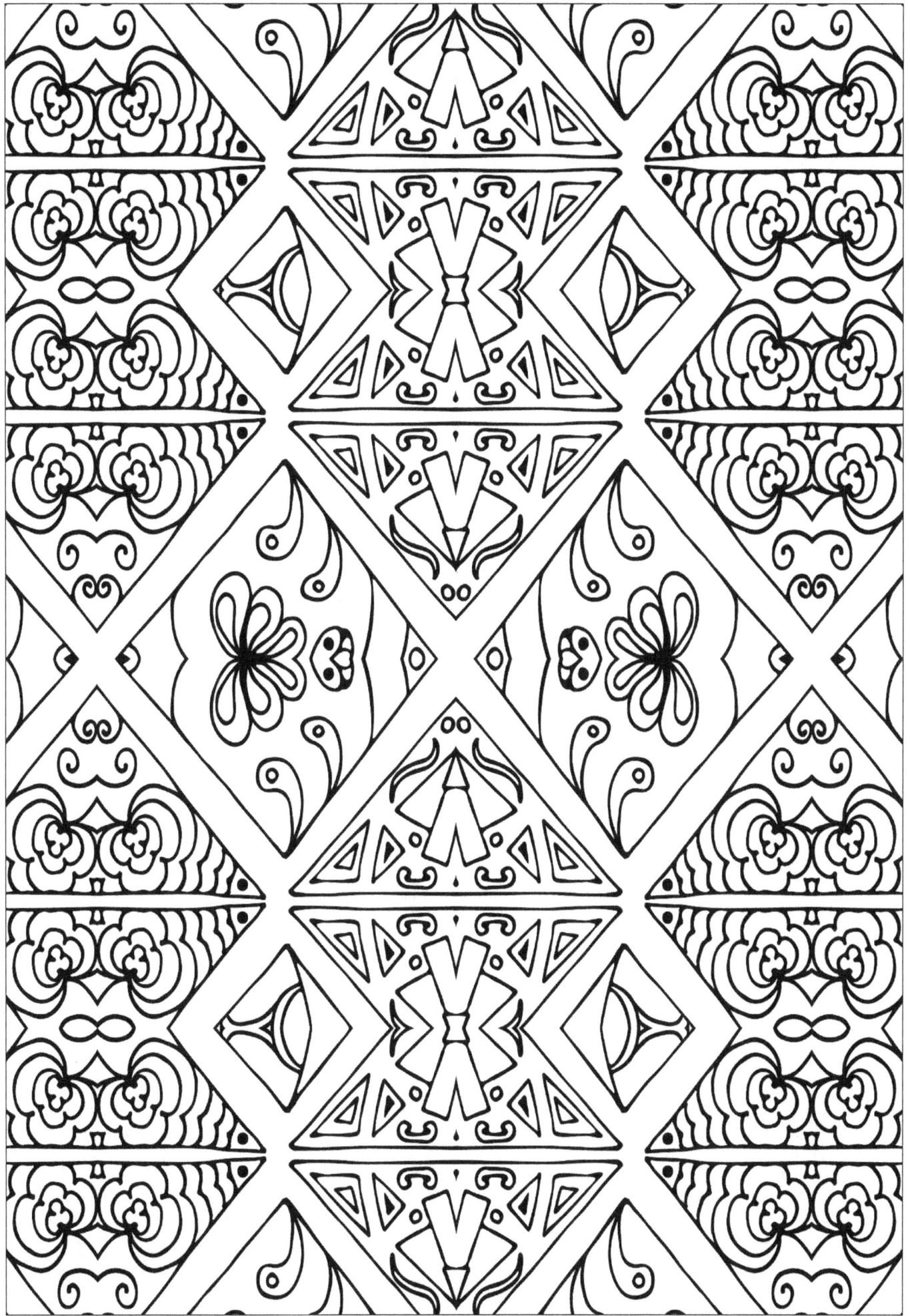

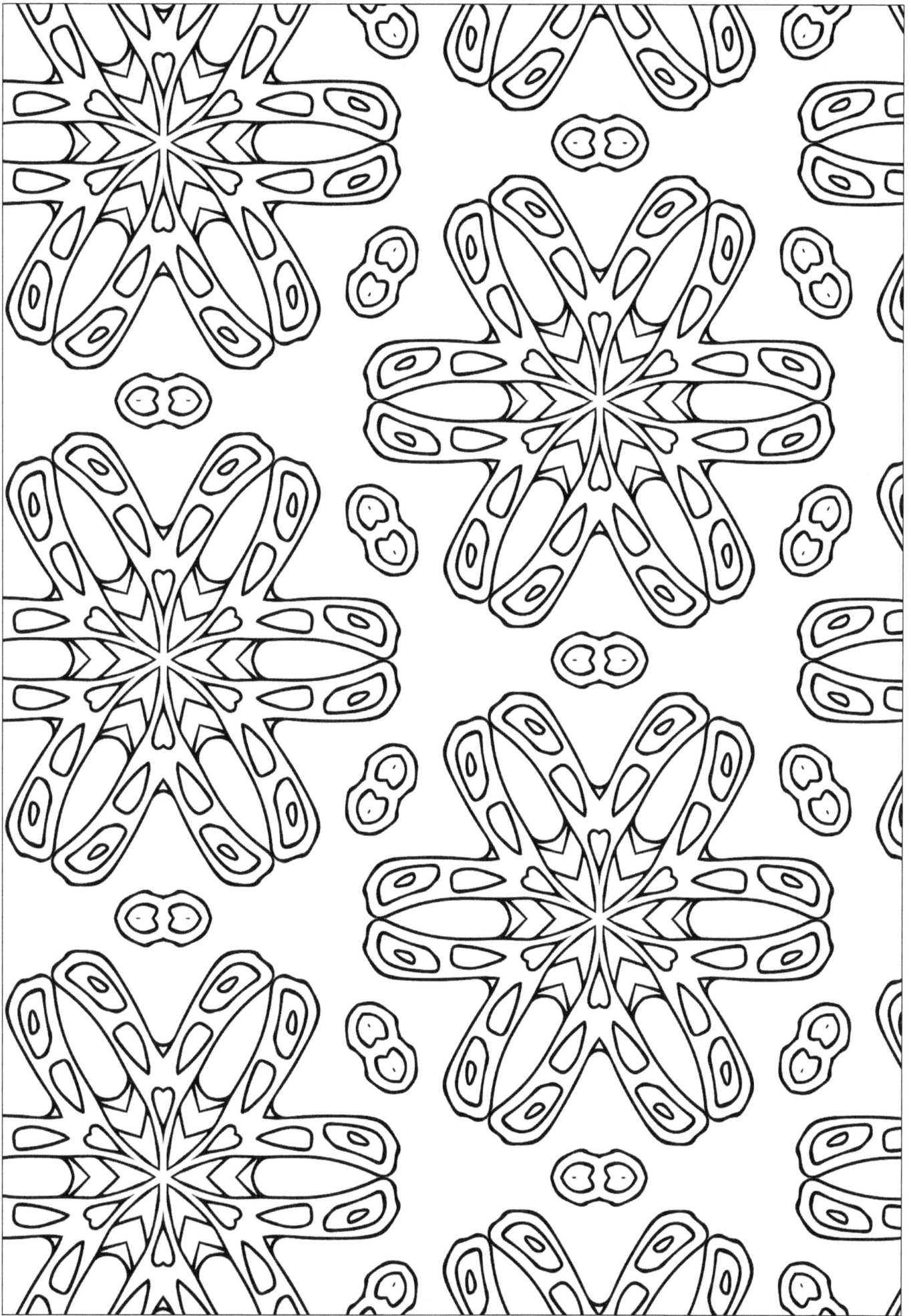

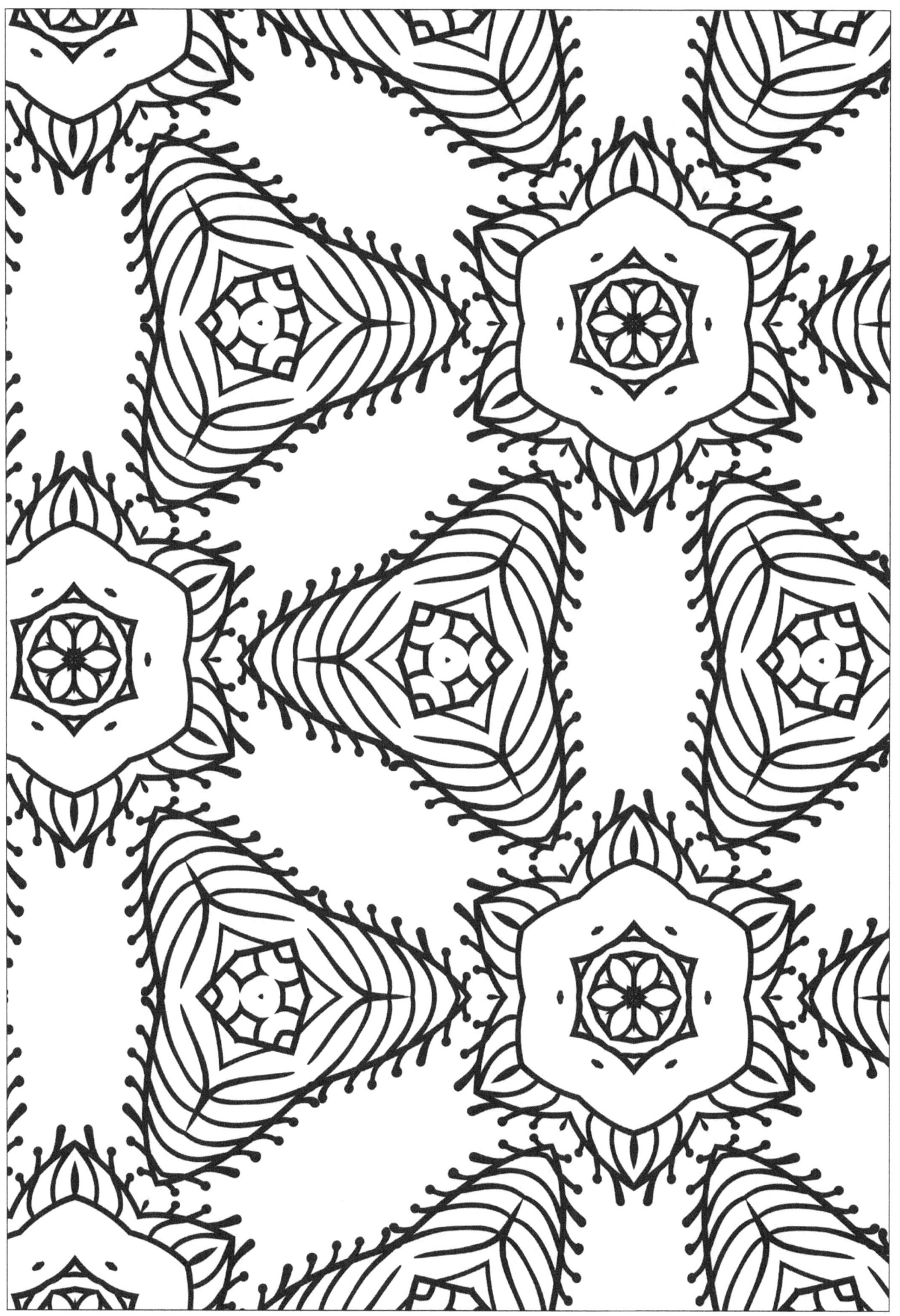

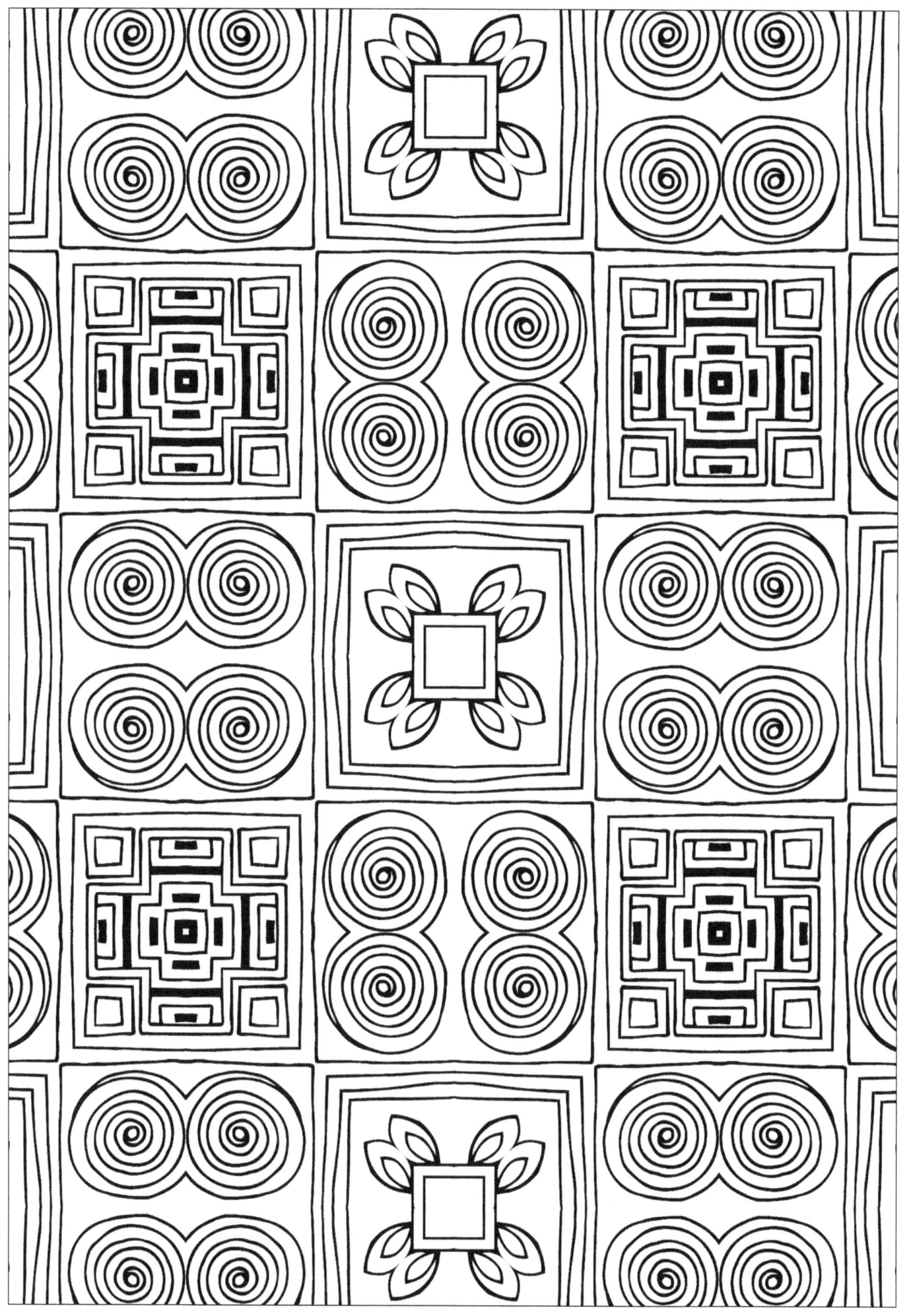

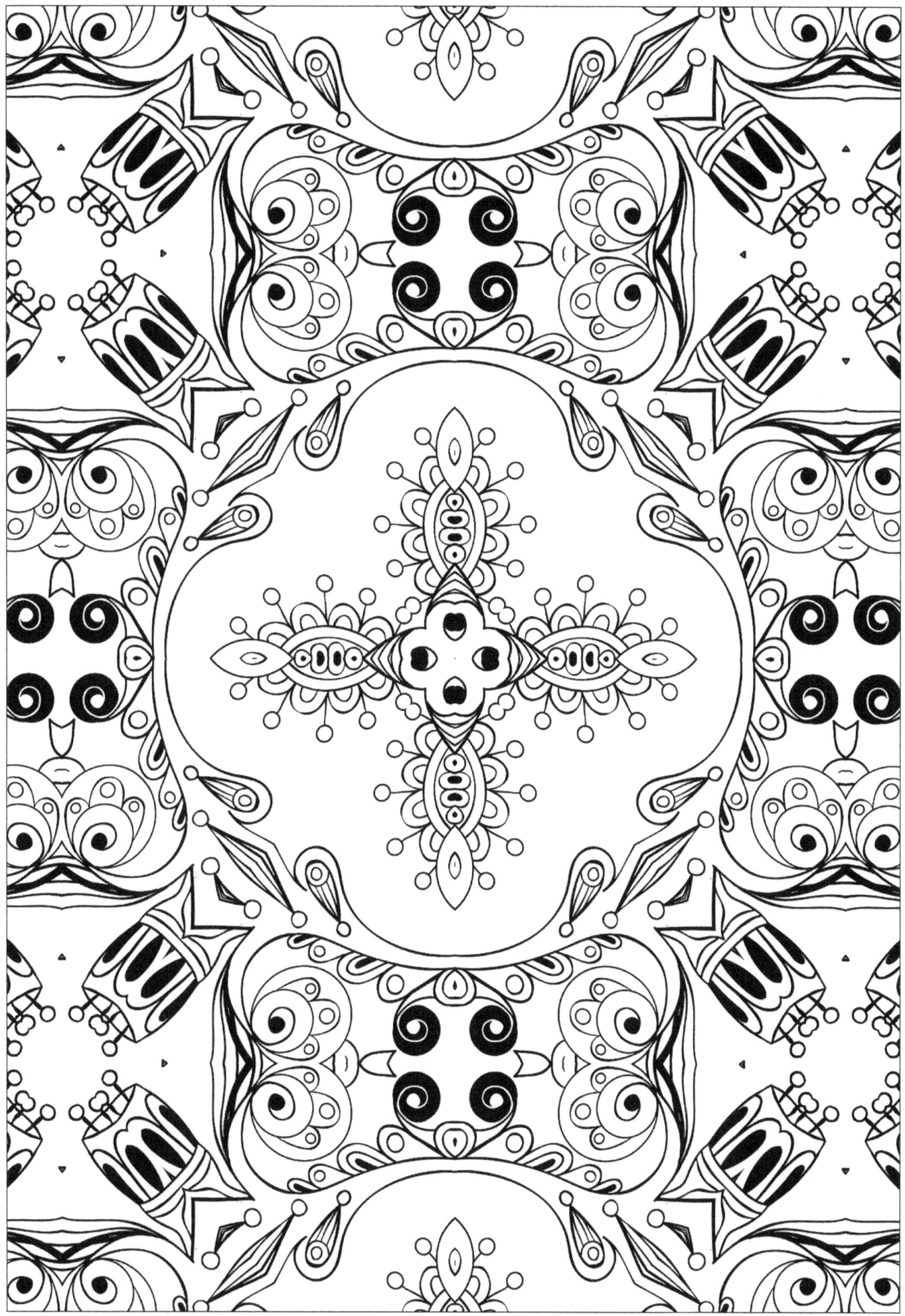

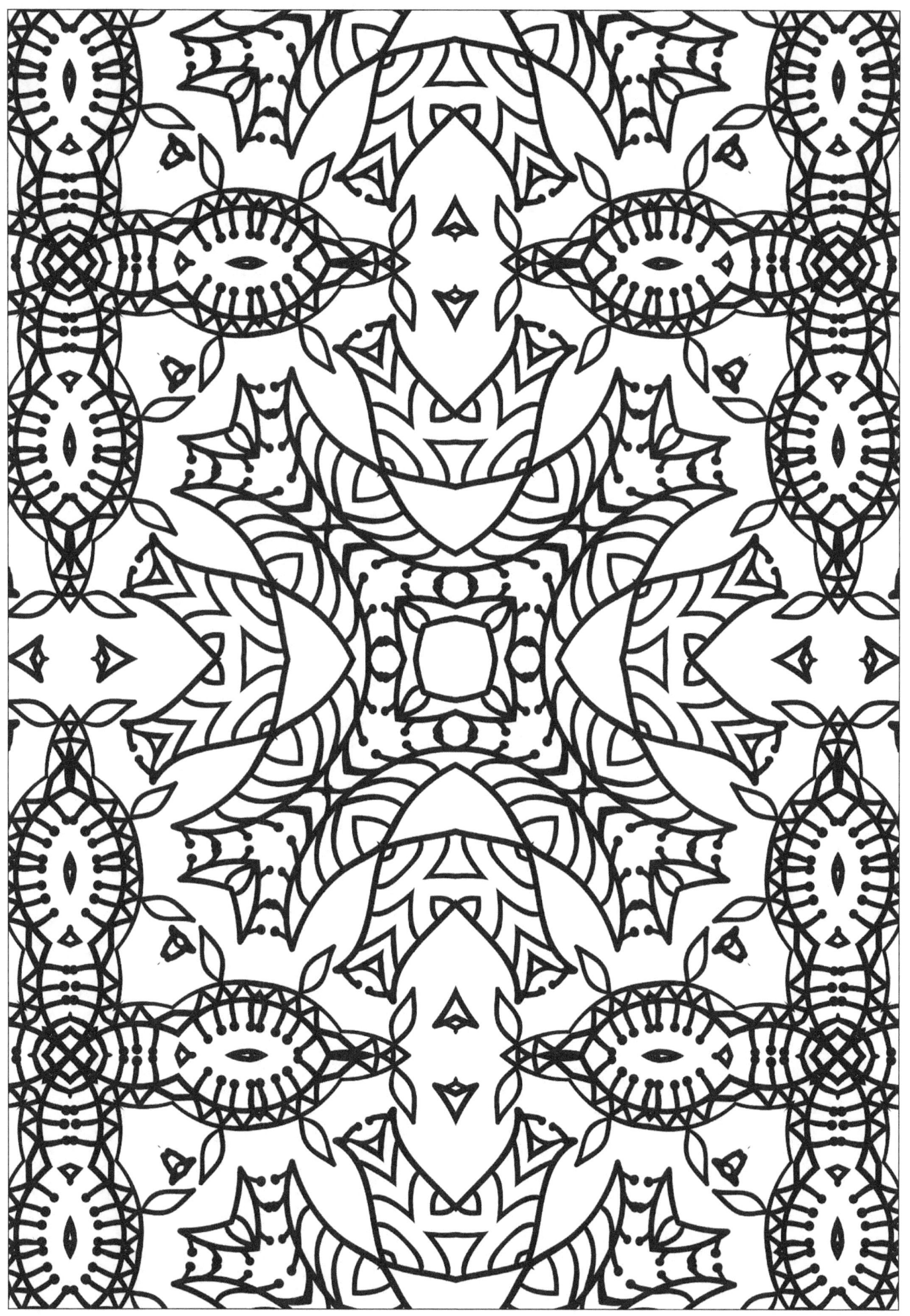

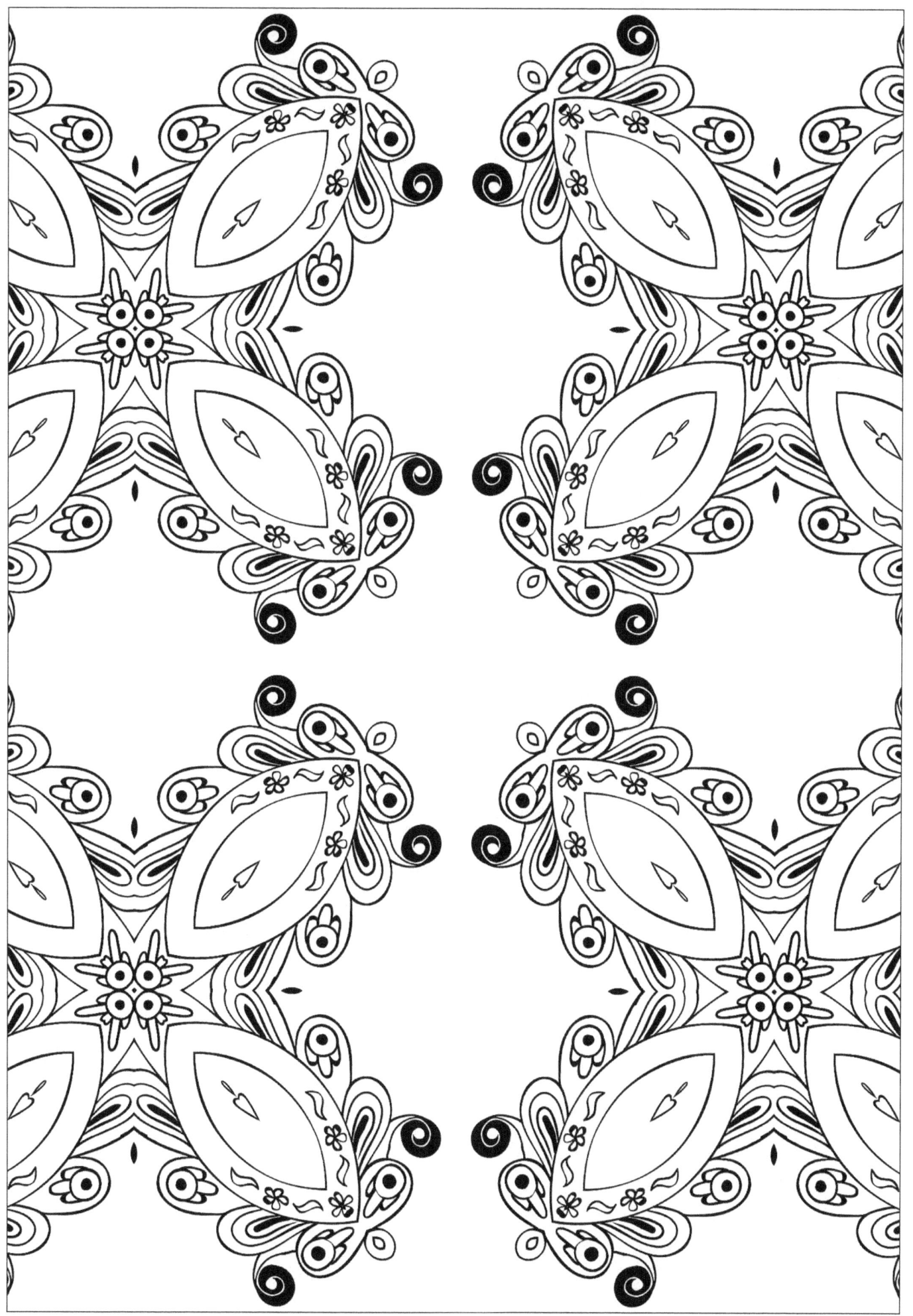

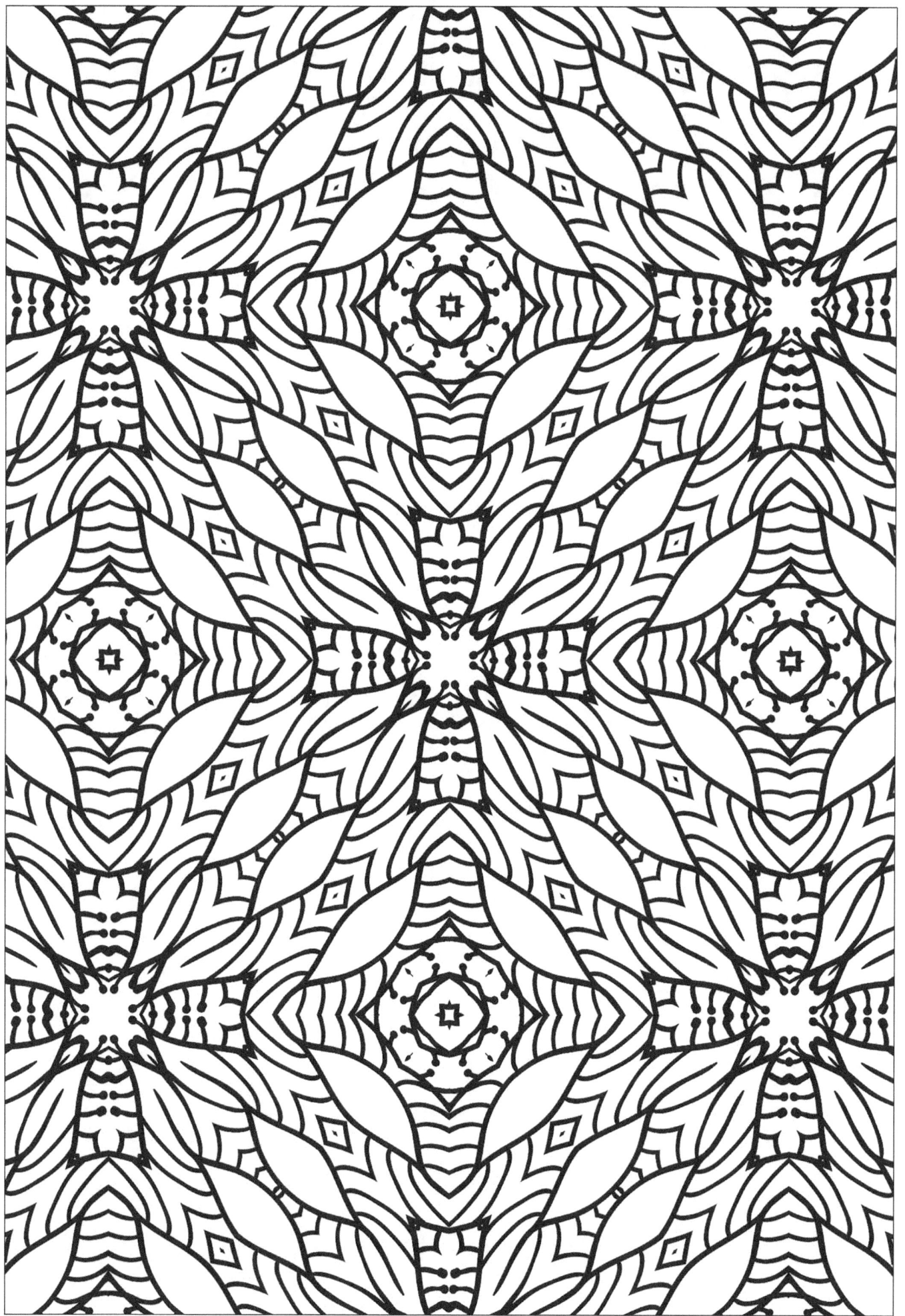

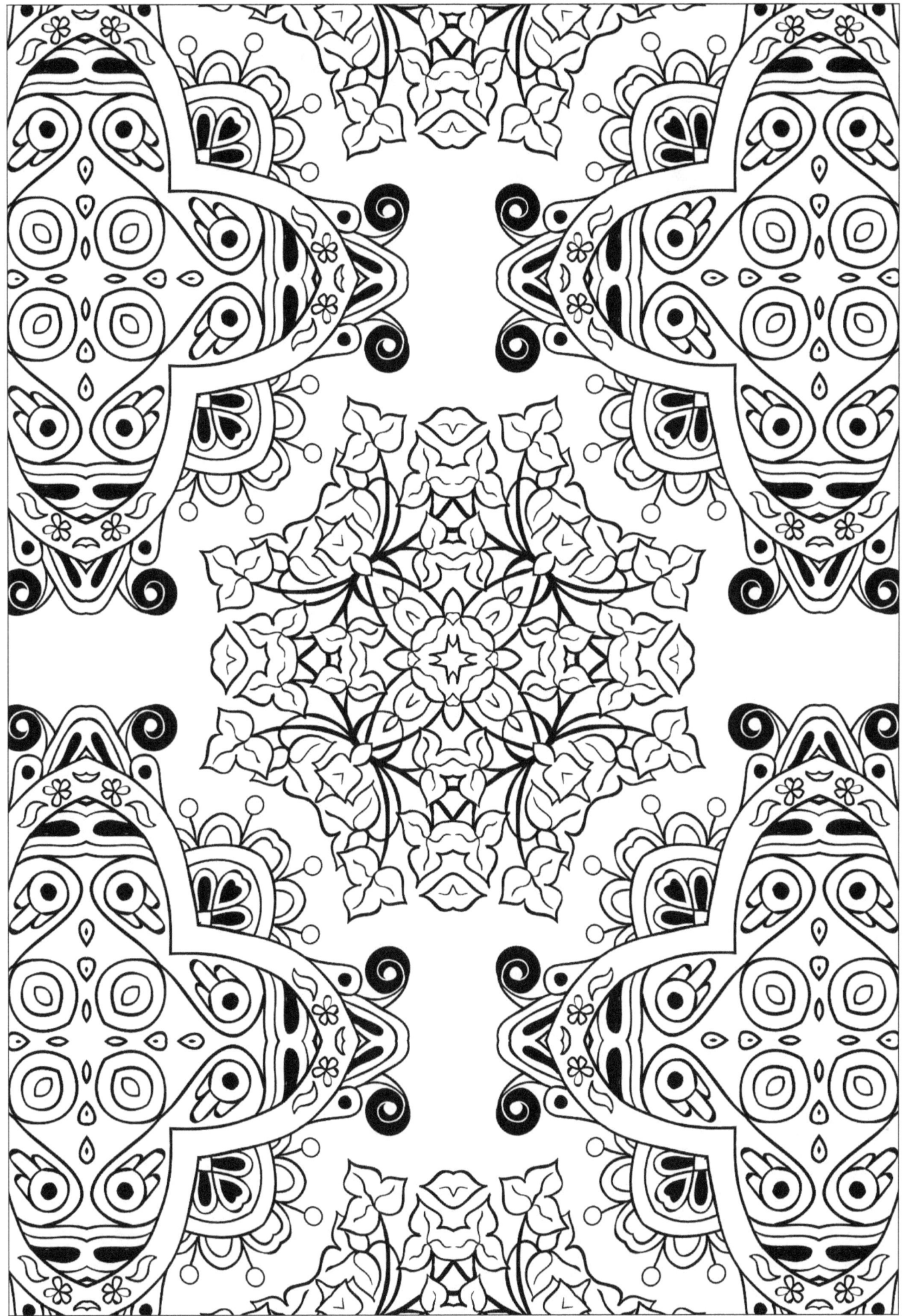

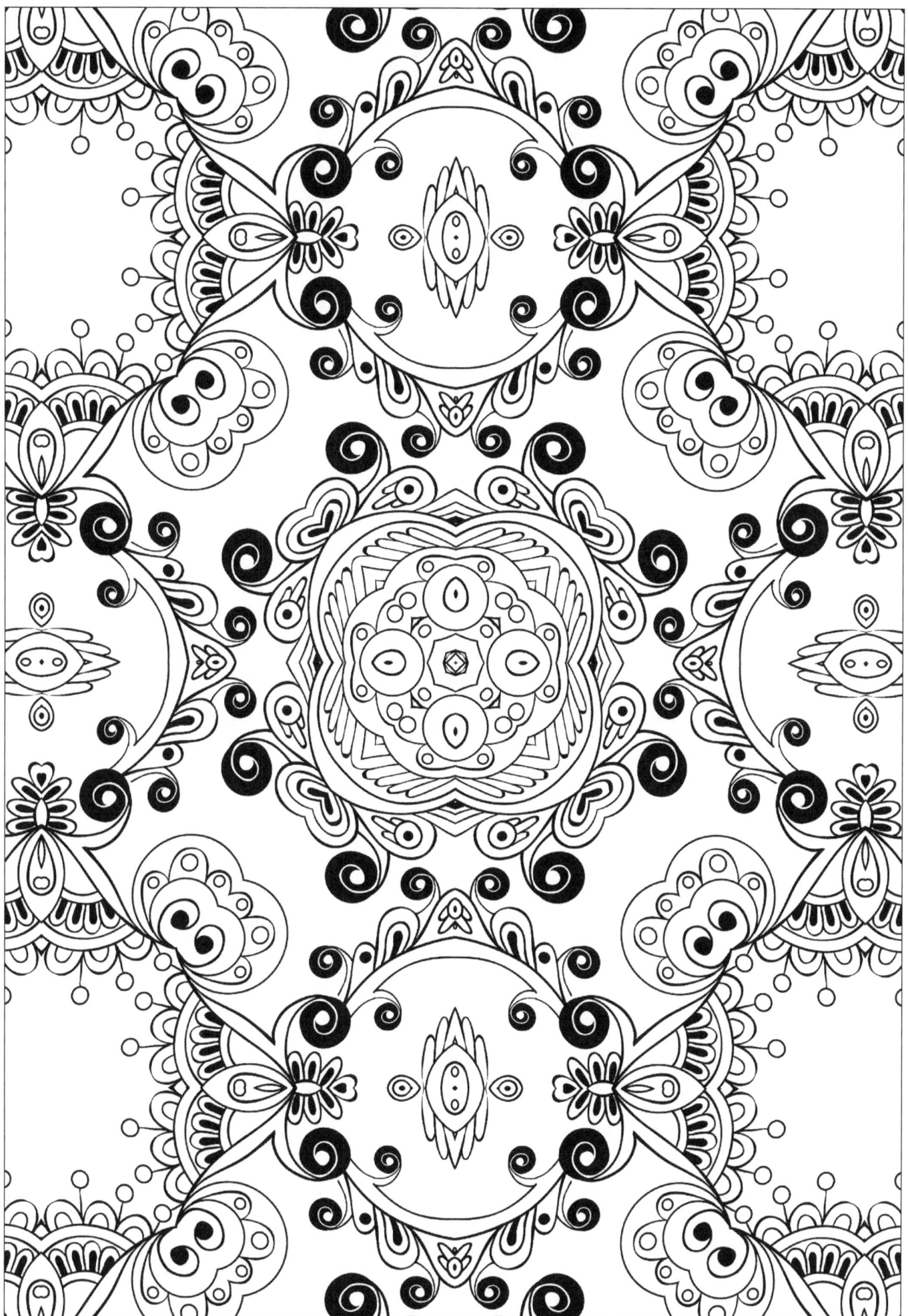

Want FREE Adult Coloring Patterns delivered straight to your inbox?

As a special thank you for downloading this Coloring Book for Adults we would like to give you free coloring patterns each week, delivered straight into your email inbox.

We would also like to keep you informed of our latest book releases, special discounts and related offers!

Just type the following link into your browser to join our email list today…

www.FatRobinBooks.com/free-coloring-patterns

Get the PDF version of this Book!

Get the PDF version of these patterns so you can print them out again.

Just type the website address below (all in lower case!) into your Internet Browser:

www.fatrobinbooks.com/15patterns.pdf

Loved the book?

We really hope you loved this book as much as we enjoyed creating it?

If you did, it would be absolutely fantastic if you could leave us a quick honest Amazon review. Just go to the Amazon product page for this book and click on 'Write a customer review' or Follow this Link.

Thank you and happy coloring.

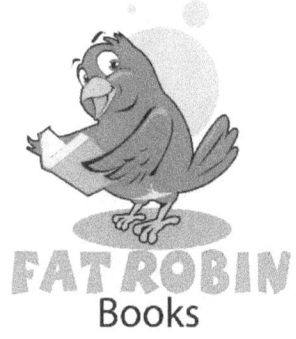

FAT ROBIN
Books